THREE POEMS

THREE POEMS

Bassacksenglish
Monopoems
Coming(s) Together

Richard Kostelanetz

Dedicated to John Ashbury

NYQ Books™

The New York Quarterly Foundation, Inc.
New York, New York

NYQ Books™ is an imprint of The New York Quarterly Foundation, Inc.

The New York Quarterly Foundation, Inc.
P.O. Box 2015
Old Chelsea Station
New York, NY 10113

www.nyqbooks.org

www.richardkostelanetz.com

Portions of the concluding text have appeared in a Runaway Spoon chapbook (2003) that is still available from its publisher (Pt. Charlotte, FL) and are reprinted here with permission.

First Edition

Layout and design by John Also Bennett

Cover photo of Richard Kostelanetz by Mary-Jo Kline

Library of Congress Control Number: 2011944481

ISBN: 978-1-935520-49-8

A principal difference between poetry and fiction, even at the avant-garde extremes, is that the latter implies narrative and thus movement from one place to another, even if the fiction is only one word long, while poetry strives for concentration of image and effect. These poems, unlike my stories, should be published, without full stops (aka "periods"). All realize poetic quality and thus esthetic weight wholly within themselves.

One recurring theme of my poetry has been the discovery of mysteries within words—within English language.

BASSACKENGLISH

AXIT
YENV
ADAT
ISTHE
SUEIS
TEXIS
EALID
LAVAI
IUMOP
ISHAM
TENOF
MOPIU
TADUL
RAZEB
EREED
ARTHE
REDOC
RYEVE
GYPUD
MESHA
RUNDE

MONOPOEMS

ambiguity

wisdom

death

sign

smoking

mourning

COMING(S) TOGETHER

mass acre
massacre

who lew heat
wholewheat

be long
belong

fig u ration
figuration

out let
outlet

dig I tally
digitally

I deal
ideal

un derc over
undercover

the rapists
therapists

swee the art
sweetheart

IGINOR
TARTIS
ISTART
CRUSTI
TINSUL
HEMET
ALIVAS
SIPIDIN
ITORED
GYMAN
VENTIN
THERMI
TEXTOR
REIGNO
MASTIG
ERATTL
TENDIN
ESTOLD
RIUMAT
MINFOR
READMI
TINFAN
MINODO
GIMERE
TOPOTA
SIPIDIN

error

sigh

home

perception

sight

home

discount

hot shot
hotshot

u ran I um
uranium

hero in
heroin

ass ass I nation
assassination

relation ships
relationships

bra in
brain

ser vice man
serviceman

re search
research

re as on
reason

test ify
testify

coin age
coinage

cel lop hane
cellophane

be witch
bewitch

RAGEMI

APAYAP

IMULIST

APTORC

ACHEAP

ISTHES

EABJUR

ASONAT

NODOMI

LEINHA

BUEDIM

REDHAT

ATASON

RAPPEA

BADVER

CAPEES

SCANVA

TESENA

HOSPAT

SPIREIN

DENTAR

CHORAN

NORPHA

DABSUR

NUNBOR

DEDECA

finale

guts

eternity

limits

enough

soul

perfume

re spi rat or
respirator

fro zen
frozen

re put at ion
reputation

to day
today

cat a comb
catacomb

be came
became

re gist rant
registrant

a venue
avenue

as ton I shed
astonished

night mare
nightmare

red ed ic ate
rededicate

ram rod
ramrod

fig u ration
figuration

GREEDE

DABOAR

HEREAD

LEGAMB

SHEROE

SPATHO

STEEME

SURDAB

SYCHOP

TABRUP

TAGHAS

TANTEX

TECHAS

TEXTAN

TINSIGH

SINSIDE

SIGNTIN

HIBITEX

VOLESIN

THEMAM

ERIMINT

TINSPEC

GEMANA

LENAME

NABANA

LLIDECO

sin

paraphernalia

moribund

chaos

hysteria

reason

reappraise

reapp raise
reappraise

pur cha sing
purchasing

not ions
notions

in sur gent
insurgent

avail able
available

comb I nation
combination

ham strings
hamstrings

ove rex pose
overexpose

fort night
fortnight

co in cide
coincide

acre age
acreage

ass u me
assume

con son ants
consonants

NOREGA
APETUNI
TIONOVA
IMISMAN
LETACTI
RICHOST
REARLIE
INGEVEN
MINTERI
TAPRICO
ISODEEP
RANSWE
NUTOPIA
RESINCE
ISANALY
LESTERI
GOTISME
TIMPLAN
MENTAIL
JURIESIN
ESTHIGH
MACUME
STAGAIN
TAGAINS
BITERAR
PIGRAME

smithereens

honesty

okay

sickness

sleep

howling

alone

rat her
rather

ob lite rate
obliterate

there fore
therefore

labor a tory
laboratory

laun dry
laundry

ma the ma tics
mathematics

forgot ten
forgotten

or gas mic
orgasmic

humming birds
hummingbirds

hog wash
hogwash

car a pace
carapace

thresh old
threshold

forget table
forgettable

OPIANUT
MEGOTIS
MADIPLO
TAILMEN
CANGELI
MATHEIS
UISHANG
AGRINCH
ERNALET
HANGUIS
NAPERSO
ULENTOP
MADILEM
LINKWEL
MIRALAD
ORPEDOT
LEAPOST
HEISMAT
TAGAINS
DORSEEN
ORAGEST
APESTAN
HLETEAT
LENTOPU
EBACLED
ESSAGEM

dishonesty

oxymoron

corpulence

privilege

convergence

gay

docile

op port unity
opportunity

char coal
charcoal

auto no my
autonomy

post card
postcard

nut rit io us
nutritious

spar row
sparrow

mul tip lied
multiplied

down town
downtown

jan it or
janitor

for gave
forgave

arm a dillo
armadillo

pro gram
program

phe no men on
phenomenon

CLOSEEN
LADMIRA
LAPPARE
COLYTEA
OSSUMOP
LECHORA
ASSAGEM
BLIVIONO
CETATEA
ATEURAM
BEDIATRI
GESTRAN
AGRAMAN
PARTRAM
AMANTAD
CHANTEN
NOTTOMA
DOMENAB
NABANDO
CRABBINI
EWELFAR
GEARRAN
DUNHEAR
KABAZOO
LABYSMA
ORNADOT

harmony

smack

vanity

defunct

untitled

patience

libido

muse um
museum

mo noch rome
monochrome

a live
alive

he sit ate
hesitate

prim rose
primrose

a mer I can
american

no mad
nomad

us u ally
usually

pop u list
populist

out line
outline

ass u age
assuage

person ally
personally

auto ma ton
automaton

MACRONY
HERENOW
MAMALGA
MATRAUM
MENTOME
EGRALINT
NUNKNOW
EATTITUD
ISTASTED
RAMATEU
ERATICOP
RANGEAR
RANGEST
UREVENT
RANOTHE
RODECOR
ROUTDOO
RUMBLEG
SAPROPO
SAULTAS
SEENDOR
SHEYELA
TIMISMOP
TAURYES
TYPOVER
THATCHE

harmony

smack

vanity

defunct

untitled

patience

libido

up on
upon

invest I gate
investigate

me lanc holy
melancholy

just ify
justify

pro men ade
promenade

ma gist rate
magistrate

slip shod
slipshod

so met me
sometime

deter gents
detergents

pass I on
passion

lou is I an an
louisianan

a gent
agent

in divi dual
individual

TOUTCAS

TRAMPAN

TRUSTEN

TOPTIMIS

TUREVEN

ULUSCUM

TONYMAN

ASSINASS

TIFACTAR

UGABOOB

TREPEDIN

THELIPOR

REINQUIX

THEDONIS

LETERRIB

TIPODEAN

DIDSPLEN

METIRESO

IRESOMET

DOLENTIN

ISAGREED

IFACTART

TADAMAN

THESITAN

YETERNIT

OTIQUEER

logocentrism

style

congruency

dehortation

detritus

jazz

fright

key note
keynote

in cum bent
incumbent

ser vices
services

el sew here
elsewhere

inde finite
indefinite

in it I ate
initiate

me di ate
mediate

em phases
emphases

geog rap her
geographer

paint boxes
paintboxes

fi lib us ter
filibuster

whole some
wholesome

ey eg lasses
eyeglasses

BELIEFUN
TONISHAS
UERILLAG
DIOCREME
COATRAIN
HASTONIS
ITAGEHER
ROUTSIDE
HERENTIN
FORMEDIN
TIGNORAN
RIMPROPE
YEASTERL
ICEPILEPT
MAPHORIS
TEESCALA
SNOBODIE
NORANTIG
TRUESTIN
DADMITTE
ROBSERVE
SITANTHE
HORISMAP
ESMOLASS
LESTRADD
ISTRICART

a muse
amuse

vent I late
ventilate

auto biography
autobiography

ex one rate
exonerate

pop u late
populate

pastor ale
pastorale

en terp rise
enterprise

so me one
someone

awe some
awesome

in fat u ate
infatuate

ball rooms
ballrooms

act u ally
actually

ed it or ship
editorship

bullseye

it

radiance

schwarmerei

smells

innuendo

blessing

disco u rage
discourage

deter mined
determined

de live ring
delivering

cong reg ate
congregate

asp halt
asphalt

comp at riot
compatriot

ban kruptcy
bankruptcy

i so late
isolate

bela boring
belaboring

ass emb lies
assemblies

cock sure
cocksure

cat e gory
category

do min ant
dominant

TOPPONEN
ANTABUND
ARMONICH
TALPHABE
ASMUCHIN
NOCENTIN
BSOLUTEA
CANARCHI
CHAPPROA
ATEOPERA
COMIUMEN
ANGAROOK
AMENTORN
ERESONAT
ERNETYET
GEMARRIA
ASSACREM
LETHORAP
GYPEDAGO
MONISHAD
HALTHOUG
LEDERIGIB
NETROMBO
ANORAMAP
NUMBRAPE
TERVIEWIN

hand some
handsome

ant it he sis
antithesis

am bass ador
ambassador

He brew
Hebrew

a band oning
abandoning

tran slate
translate

uns killed
unskilled

un derp aid
underpaid

unc hanged
unchanged

ult im at um
ultimatum

ma chin ist
machinist

pen chant
penchant

te leg rams
telegrams

cheers

epoxy

intuition

skyscraper

prestige

optimism

blindness

syn the tic
synthetic

my stery
mystery

sto new are
stoneware

sop homo re
sophomore

or phaned
orphaned

so lic it or
solicitor

rest o ring
restoring

re qui site
requisite

re hear sal
rehearsal

rear range
rearrange

gall ant
gallant

I so late
isoslate

real igned
realigned

DIRRECTIN
NUNBROKE
TRENCHEN
ONSENSEN
VECTIVEIN
ORABLEAD
PARENTAP
ITIATIVEIN
POSTATEA
PUTATEAM
RANCESTO
LIVIOUSOB
RANTEATE
REAPERTU
CATHEISTI
DENDUMAD
LIGATORAL
NAMENTOR
LEVERSATI
SMARTOUT
SNOTABLE
GUMENTAR
ENTIALESS
THYPNOTIS
TINTELLEC
SUNAWARE

pube scent
pubescent

pro tot ype
prototype

pre cip ice
precipice

ear shot
earshot

dec or ate
decorate

sun days
sundays

pol ice man
policeman

six teen
sixteen

phy sic ian
physician

enig ma
enigma

pa rag raph
paragraph

eventuate
event u ate

tee total
teetotal

avarice

telescope

philosophy

confidence

realism

majesty

labyrinth

or thod oxy
orthodoxy

muni cipal
municipal

mon i to red
monitored

mis beg ot ten
misbegotten

mi crip hone
microphone

delight fully
delightfully

me tap hors
metaphors

a sleep
asleep

me an de red
meandered

in disc rim I nation
indiscrimination

pen tho use
penthouse

fund a mentalism
fundamentalism

success or ship
successorship

TARMAMEN
VESTORSIN
REDISFIGU
TEASEMEN
TEXTREMIS
THINDSIGH
TRIBUTEAT
TORNAMEN
TINGUSHEX
ARRICADEB
TOVERNIGH
STABLISHE
MAPANORA
MISTICEAR
LESSENTIA
JAMAHARA
PEPROTOTY
OVEREIGNS
GUNDERLIN
AIDUNDERP
TANTITRUS
ANDSCAPEL
CERTAINUN
ATHOLOGYP
BELLISHEM
TESTIMULA

sit u at I on
situation

psycho logical
psychological

pro life ration
proliferation

su stains
sustains

in sign ifi cant
insignificant

a gain
again

hy pot he sizing
hypothesizing

care fully
carefully

cry stall I zing
crystallizing

out look
outlook

counter at tack
counterattack

be cause
because

con side ring
considering

remnant

celibacy

extreme

fog

aphrodisia

insouciance

deficit

ass ass I nation
assassination

peas ants
peasants

undi mini shed
undiminished

surp rises
surprises

sat is faction
satisfaction

stale mate
stalemate

temp era mental
temperamental

il lust ration
illustration

a corn
acorn

il leg it I mate
illegitimate

gras shopper
grasshopper

disc rim I mate
discrimimate

forget fully
forgetfully

BITRAGEAR
CAPABLEIN
ONGSIDEAL
TABSTINEN
THOUSEBOA
CHITECTAR
RACISMOST
DERLINGUN
LETEAKETT
TEANECTDO
ETHEREFOR
GERMESSEN
TESTALEMA
TUNDERFOO
EFORETHER
GLUMBERIN
VENTUREAD
HENOMENAP
ANGUTANOR
IMATUMULT
LAUGHTONS
MENTAPART
ERWARDAFT
MEWHOLESO
VEINNOVATI
DAFTERWAR

author I tar ian
authoritarian

for bid
forbid

ho met own
hometown

con science
conscience

char is ma
charisma

bee hives
beehives

at ten u ate
attenuate

in vocation
invocation

disc over able
discoverable

after math
aftermath

spec I men
specimen

kid dies
kiddies

coun terp arts
counterparts

all-there

through

chump

noise

retrograde

filial

measure

pen ile
penile

am bi dextrous
ambidextrous

flu or es cent
fluorescent

chi rop ractor
chiropractor

phosp hate
phosphate

cat as trophes
catastrophes

loco motives
locomotives

bell ige rants
belligerents

in sane
insane

ma hog any
mahogany

an tit he tic al
antithetical

special ties
specialties

re pet it I on
repetition

TERPRISEEN
DAMPERSAN
OPAUSEMEN
OTHEGEMAP
PARATUSAP
PEARCHETY
PERSANDAM
REACHOVER
NOVATIVEIN
REDEPARTU
TENJOYMEN
REDRUGSTO
RUCHUREST
SOURELEVE
ICARITHMAT
REEMENTAG
TAGREEMEN
ISAPOTHEOS
DAMEMORAN
TAMENDMEN
VESTMENTIN
SEWAREHOU
WHELMOVER
BETICALPHA
AREHOUSEW
INUENDODIM

protest ants
protestants

in do lent
indolent

prose cuting
prosecuting

me mor I am
memoriam

car rots
carrots

pa tri arch al
patriarchal

on to logical
ontological

infer red
inferred

ob sole scent
obsolescent

no net he less
nonetheless

rein deer
reindeer

nigh ting ale
nightingale

mini stering
ministering

since

romantic

panache

heaven

undervelop

poem

antinomy

merit or I o us
meritorious

make shift
makeshift

men tali ties
mentalities

ram page
rampage

ma trim on I al
matrimonial

stub born
stubborn

mad rig a ling
madrigaling

bed fellows
bedfellows

in car nation
incarnation

high way
highway

lu mine scent
luminescent

under go
undergo

in ha bit ants
inhabitants

BISHOPARCH
SISHYPOTHE
ISCLOSURED
DEARMENTEN
DERCOVERUN
DICRAFTHAN
EATMOSPHER
GETHERALTO
GYPSYCHOLO
HEAPOSTROP
ISTOCRATAR
MENTEQUIPT
MENTHUSIAS
MENTENTRAP
MOSPHEREAT
NARCHISTAN
NETRAMPOLI
NUNDERTAKE
ODIDACTAUT
OSTROPHEAP
POCALYPSEA
PONTMENTAP
PROBRIUMOP
RAMPOLINET
TWITCHCRAF
STRUMENTIN

to wed
towed

in fan try man
infantryman

rot ate
rotate

in dig nation
indignation

wind mills
windmills

in a lien able
inalienable

star lets
starlets

her ring bone
herringbone

dead line
deadline

harp si chord
harpsichord

plain tiff
plaintiff

grand fat her
grandfather

port folio
portfolio

tongue

equality

transparency

loud

modular

supreme

spunk

prop a gate
propagate

child hood
childhood

fel lows hips
fellowships

disc overies
discoveries

me gal o man I a
megalomania

demon strate
demonstrate

co spon so red
cosponsored

sign ify
signify

an glop ho bia
anglophobia

ant is la very
antislavery

a rose
arose

con cent rate
concentrate

app rent ices
apprentices

TAGONISTAN
YESPECIALL
THUSIASMEN
TICULATEAR
TINVESTMEN
TERNATIVEAL
TRANEOUSEX
TENGAGEMEN
TOMBMENTEN
VEALTERNATI
YAPOTHECAR
TITLEMENTEN
ACHRONISMAN
ADVERTENTIN
DIFFERENTIN
TINADVERTEN
DUSTRIOUSIN
GYMETHODOLO
MENTENTITLE
RAMPITHEATE
RAVAGANTEXT
TOXICATINGIN
SASSINATEAS
TENCHANTMEN
ITECTUREARCH
RANGEMENTAR

phos phor es cent
phosphorescent

auto bio graphy
autobiography

rot is series
rotisseries

arch I pel ago
archipelago

war mish
warmish

car to grap her
cartographer

profess or
professor

app rent ice
apprentice

vigil ante
vigilante

stabilize
stab I lize

novice
no vice

dread fully
dreadfully

authors hip
authorship

orthodoxy

tenacity

ghostliness

cliché

land

epitaph

predisposition

TINSIGNIFICAN
CIRCLEMENTEN
ISHONORABLED
MENTUNEMPLOY
OMEMCLATUREN
TANNOUNCEMEN
TESTRANGEMEN
ABLISHMENTEST
MENTESTABLISH
MENTENCOURAGE

I shall not
make poetry
remembering
my travels
to exotic
lands.

I shall not
make poetry
about my
ancestors,
illustrious
or not, and
thus my pur-
portedly
particular
inheritance.

I shall not make poetry praising children – mine or others (or myself as a child).

I shall not make poetry about sexism or nuclear war or un- p o p u l a r politicians.

I shall not make poetry meant to be read aloud to an appre-ciative audience.

I shall not make poetry about birth or death, or any other subject best left to professional theologians and philosophers.

I shall not make poetry in imitation of any con- sciousness, primitive or other- wise alien to my own.

I shall not

make poetry

addressing the

wondrous

nature of

wonderful

nature.

I shall not m a k e p o e t r y a b o u t m e n t a l distress, e i t h e r r e a l o r imagined.

I shall not

make poetry

designed to

be imitated

by submissive

students.

I shall not make poetry based upon anecdotes or pretentions to precious empathy.

I shall not make poetry whose implicit purpose, ideally recognized only by a few, would be to flatter V e r y Important P o e t s.

I shall not make poetry that resembles, even superficially, any "poetry" that anyone else has written.

Individual entries on **RICHARD KOSTELANETZ** *appear in* A Reader's Guide to Twentieth-Century Writers, The Merriam-Webster Encyclopedia of Literature, Webster's Dictionary of American Authors, The HarperCollins Reader's Encyclopedia of American Literature, Baker's Biographical Dictionary of Musicians, *and* the Britannica.com, *among other distinguished directories. Otherwise, he survives in New York, where he was born, unemployed and thus overworked.*

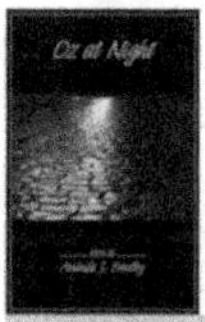

six rivers
EVERY THING SO SERIOUSLY
Yellow Plum Season

Voluptuous Gloom
The Puzzle Master
TOURIST
0.174

www.ingramcontent.com/pod-product-compliance
Lightning Source LLC
LaVergne TN
LVHW051849080426
835512LV00018B/3163